HEINEMANN STATE STUDIES

All Around Illinois

Regions and Resources

Andrew Santella

Heinemann Library
Chicago, Illinois

© 2003 Reed Educational & Professional Publishing
Published by Heinemann Library,
an imprint of Reed Educational & Professional
Publishing, Chicago, Illinois

Customer Service 888-454-2279

Visit our website at www.heinemannlibrary.com

Designed by Heinemann Library
Page layout by Depke Design
Printed and bound in the United States by Lake
Book Manufacturing, Inc.

07 06 05 04 03
10 9 8 7 6 5 4 3 2 1

**Library of Congress
Cataloging-in-Publication Data**
Santella, Andrew.
  All around Illinois : regions and resources / by
Andrew Santella.
      p. cm. -- (State studies)
Includes bibliographical references and index.
  ISBN 1-40340-007-5 (HC), 1-40340-568-9 (Pbk)
  1. Illinois--Geography--Juvenile literature.
[1. Illinois--Geography.] I. Title. II. State studies
(Heinemann Library (Firm))
  F541.8 .S26 2002
  917.73--dc21
                                        2002000795

Acknowledgments
The author and publishers are grateful to the
following for permission to reproduce copyright
material:

Cover photographs by (TL-TR): Corbis; Corbis;
Robert Lifson/Heinemann Library; Lowell
Georgia/Corbis; (bottom) Richard Day/Daybreak
Imagery

pp. 4, 22, 24, 26, 35B Robert Lifson/Heinemann
Library; pp. 5, 8, 11, 13, 16, 19, 21, 29, 30, 37,
39 maps.com/Heinemann Library; p. 6 Bob and Ira
Spring/Stock Connection/Picture Quest; pp. 7, 14,
17, 18, 20, 44 James P. Rowan; p. 9 Heinemann
Library; p. 10 Ben Weddle/Midwestock; p. 12T
Sandy Felsenthal/Corbis; p. 12B David Derr; p. 15
Corbis; pp. 23T, 25, 35T, 36 Illinois Department of
Commerce and Community Affairs; pp. 23B, 33
Milt Mann/Cameramann International; p. 27
Duane Zehr/Bradley University; p. 28 U.S Army
Corps of Engineers; p. 31 Fred Jewell/AP Wide
World Photo; p. 32 Deere & Company; p. 34
Layne Kennedy/Corbis; p. 38 AP/Wide World
Photos; p. 40 Richard Day/Daybreak Imagery;
p. 41 Kim Karpeles/Midwestock; p. 42T Robert
Glusic/PhotoDisc; p. 42B Granite City Division,
National Steel Corporation; p. 43 Charles Rex
Arbogast/AP Photo; p. 45 Grant Heilman
Photography.

Special thanks to Tom Schwartz of the Illinois
Historic Preservation Agency, for his expert help
and advice on the series.

Every effort has been made to contact copyright
holders of any material reproduced in this book.
Any omissions will be rectified in subsequent
printings if notice is given to the publisher.

Some words are shown in bold, **like this.**
You can find out what they mean by looking
in the glossary.

Contents

An Introduction to Illinois

Anyone who has taken a trip across Illinois knows most of the state is flat. Fields of corn and soybeans stretch along roads as far as the eye can see. Those crops have helped feed the world for more than 150 years.

However, there is much more to Illinois than flat farmland. Illinois is 385 miles (620 kilometers) long and 218 miles (351 kilometers) wide. Within its borders, a person can find hills, valleys, forests, and **wetlands.** Illinois is bordered by one of the largest lakes in the world, Lake Michigan. It is also home to smaller lakes, both human-made and natural. The state contains tiny country towns and the huge city of Chicago. It supports both farms and factories. Even the weather varies greatly from northern to southern Illinois. It is a state filled with surprises and variety.

GLACIER-MADE

Much of Illinois was shaped by **glaciers.** Glaciers are huge sheets of ice that can cover hundreds of miles of land and

Until the mid–1800s, Illinois was mostly prairie land. Today, most of that prairie land has been turned into farm fields of corn and soybeans.

Illinois

Northern

Central

Southern

0   250 mi.

0   250 km

be over a mile thick. One hundred thousand years ago, glaciers began spreading south over Illinois. They covered almost all of the state. Fifteen thousand years ago, the glaciers began melting in a northerly direction.

When the glaciers disappeared they left behind a changed land. The glaciers were so heavy that they had flattened much of Illinois. Only the areas that were not covered by glaciers were not flattened, such as the northwest corner of the state. Today, rolling hills rise along the rivers there.

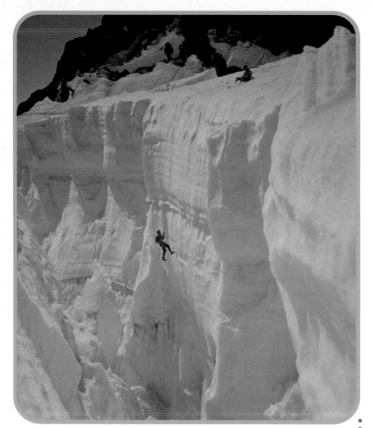

Thousands of years ago, glaciers similar to this one (above) helped shape the Illinois land. Glaciers can be as much as a mile thick, but usually only move about a foot (30 centimeters) a day.

Illinois's highest point is in Jo Daviess County. It's called Charles Mound, and is 1,235 feet (376 meters) tall.

Parts of western and southern Illinois are hilly, as well. Like northwest Illinois, these areas were not flattened by **glaciers.** Calhoun County in western Illinois has rugged, rolling **terrain.** So does southern Illinois. The Shawnee Hills of southern Illinois contain several hills that are more than 1,000 feet (305 meters) high. Southern Illinois is also home to Shawnee National Forest, the only national forest in the state. The ponderosa pine and Douglas fir trees of the forest blanket the hillsides. Most of the state, however, is a level plain about 600 feet (183 meters) above sea level.

More than 900 rivers and streams cross Illinois. Three large rivers form part of the state's borders. The Mississippi River forms the western border. The Ohio River is Illinois's southern border. The Wabash River makes up much of the state's eastern border. The Rock, Kaskaskia, Big Muddy, Illinois, and many other rivers run through the interior of the state. These rivers drain a large part of the middle United States. Water from 23 states flows through Illinois. Some flows eastward to the Atlantic Ocean, through Lake Michigan. Most flows south through the Ohio and Mississippi Rivers to the Gulf of Mexico.

Illinois is home to both natural and human-made lakes. Most human-made lakes were created by building **dams** on rivers. Illinois's largest interior lake is Carlyle Lake, near Vandalia in southern Illinois. It covers 24,580 acres (9,947 hectares). Underground water supplies, or **aquifers,** are another important source of water for the state. Underground water is pumped up through wells and used to **irrigate** farm fields and for drinking.

ILLINOIS AT WORK

Ancient glaciers left behind **minerals** that made Illinois's soil **fertile.** Today, Illinois is one of the nation's leading agricultural states. Corn and soybeans are the state's main crops. In fact, Illinois competes with Iowa for top ranking in U.S. corn and soybean production. Illinois farmers grow a variety of other crops, as well. They grow wheat, asparagus, cabbage, green beans, apples, peaches, blueberries, and other fruits and vegetables.

The Mississippi River (below) forms the western border of Illinois. People have traveled up and down the mighty Mississippi for hundreds of years. It is the second-longest river in the U.S., after the Missouri River.

Illinois Topography

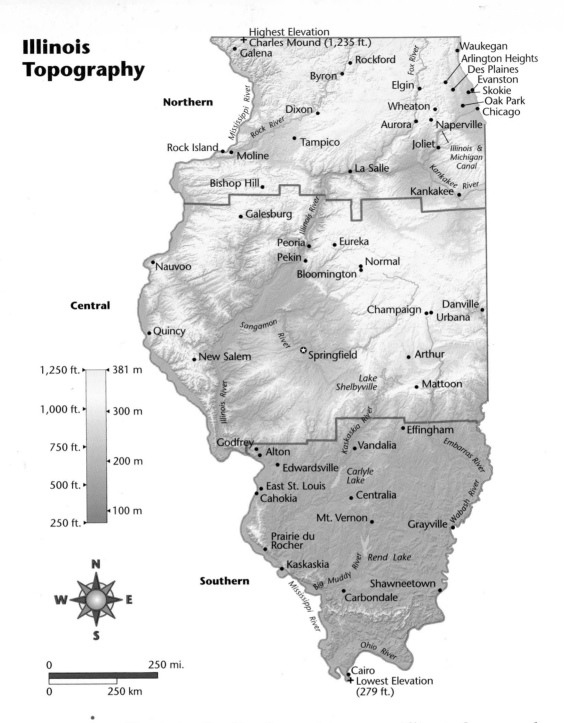

Illinois Topography map. Regions labeled Northern, Central, Southern.

Highest Elevation — Charles Mound (1,235 ft.)

Cities and features shown include:
Galena, Byron, Rockford, Waukegan, Arlington Heights, Des Plaines, Evanston, Skokie, Oak Park, Chicago, Elgin, Wheaton, Aurora, Naperville, Dixon, Tampico, Joliet, Rock Island, Moline, La Salle, Bishop Hill, Kankakee, Galesburg, Peoria, Pekin, Eureka, Normal, Bloomington, Nauvoo, Champaign, Danville, Urbana, Quincy, New Salem, Springfield, Arthur, Mattoon, Godfrey, Alton, Edwardsville, Vandalia, Effingham, East St. Louis, Cahokia, Centralia, Mt. Vernon, Grayville, Prairie du Rocher, Kaskaskia, Shawneetown, Carbondale, Cairo

Rivers and lakes: Mississippi River, Rock River, Fox River, Illinois River, Kankakee River, Illinois & Michigan Canal, Sangamon River, Lake Shelbyville, Kaskaskia River, Embarras River, Carlyle Lake, Wabash River, Rend Lake, Big Muddy River, Ohio River

Lowest Elevation (279 ft.) at Cairo

Elevation scale: 1,250 ft. / 381 m; 1,000 ft. / 300 m; 750 ft. / 200 m; 500 ft. / 100 m; 250 ft.

Compass: N, E, S, W

0 — 250 mi.
0 — 250 km

Illinois seems like mostly flatland at first, but each region actually has a variety of hills, fields, rivers, and lakes.

Illinois is a leading hog-raising state. Illinois farmers also raise sheep, poultry, and cattle for both beef and dairy products. A few farms even raise exotic birds like **ostriches** and **emus** for their meat, hides, and feathers. Many of Illinois's agricultural products are sold to other countries, or **exported.** Illinois is second in the nation in the value of exported agricultural products. The state sends about $4 billion worth of agricultural products overseas each year. Almost half the grain grown in Illinois each year is exported to other countries.

Beneath the surface of Illinois lie valuable **resources.** They include supplies of **petroleum, natural gas,** lead, and coal. Illinois has more **bituminous coal** beneath its surface than any other state. Coal is called a **fossil** fuel, because it comes from the fossilized remains of plants and animals buried more than 200 million years ago. It is also nonrenewable, which means once it runs out, we can't make more. Coal is burned to provide heat, which is used to run power plants that produce electricity.

The state's most valuable **mineral** resource is crushed stone. Other resources mined in Illinois include construction sand and gravel. Illinois is a leading producer of sand and gravel used by **industry.** Some Illinois sand is used to make glass. Illinois is also first in the production of **tripoli,** a rock used in the

The gross state product is the total value of the goods and services produced by the people of Illinois in a year. In 1999, Illinois produced 445 billion dollars worth of goods.

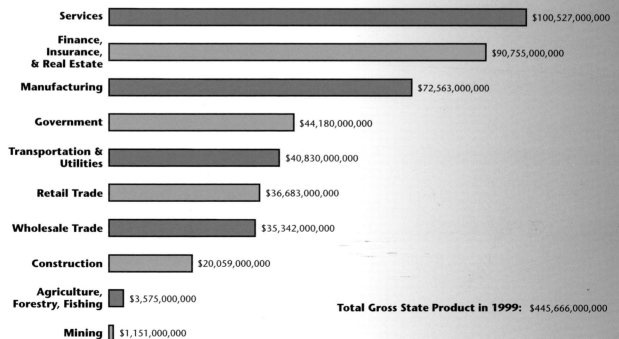

The Illinois Economy
Gross State Product (in dollars)

Services	$100,527,000,000
Finance, Insurance, & Real Estate	$90,755,000,000
Manufacturing	$72,563,000,000
Government	$44,180,000,000
Transportation & Utilities	$40,830,000,000
Retail Trade	$36,683,000,000
Wholesale Trade	$35,342,000,000
Construction	$20,059,000,000
Agriculture, Forestry, Fishing	$3,575,000,000
Mining	$1,151,000,000

Total Gross State Product in 1999: $445,666,000,000

The raising of livestock, such as hogs (right), is an important industry in Illinois. Illinois produces over 4 million head of hogs each year. Many hog farmers also grow corn, which they use to feed the hogs.

manufacturing of plastics and rubber. Illinois also produces clay and **limestone** used for building materials.

Many of Illinois's industries are related to agriculture and mining. Since the 1830s, Illinois factories have made farm equipment. Illinois is home to more than 1,000 food producing companies that turn the state's crops into food. Illinois is a leading producer of flour, syrups, cooking oils, and pet food. Food processing is the state's top manufacturing industry. Illinois is also a leading producer of cellular phones, chemicals, radios, televisions, and printed materials. Many of these products are sold to consumers in other countries. Illinois is sixth among states in the value of its **exported** goods.

Ethanol

Corn and other Illinois farm produce is used as food, of course. However, crops are also turned into a wide variety of other products. These include soap, paint, ink, wax, paper, medicines, animal feed, and glue. One of the most important products made from Illinois crops is ethanol. Ethanol is a fuel, made from corn, that is used in gasoline to help power cars and trucks. The state produces 690 million gallons (2.6 billion liters) of ethanol each year.

Illinois Resources

Natural Resources

- Coal
- Petroleum
- Stone, gravel

Agriculture

- Fruit
- Hay
- Beef
- Corn
- Poultry
- Wheat
- Dairy products
- Soybeans
- Hogs
- Sheep

Manufacturing

- Steel
- Lead
- Farm equipment
- Food products
- Electrical machinery/ equipment

0   50 mi.

0   50 km

CROSSROADS

Illinois has always been a crossroads state. It is located in the middle of the United States and near important waterways. Before trains, cars, and planes, water travel was the best way to move around. For thousands of years, Native Americans used the rivers and lakes of Illinois as highways. They paddled hundreds of miles to trade with distant neighbors. Today, large ships and **barges** travel up

Illinois has many valuable natural and human-made resources in every region. Farming is an especially important industry in Illinois.

O'Hare International Airport

Chicago's O'Hare International Airport (right) is one of the world's busiest airports. It was a factory and airfield for military planes during World War II (1939–1945), and was called Orchard Place at that time. Even though the airport is no longer called Orchard Place, its air **industry** code letters are still ORD. After the war, the city of Chicago took ownership of the land. In 1955, regular commercial flights began flying into O'Hare International Airport. The airport is named for Edward "Butch" O'Hare, a hero of World War II. He was a Navy pilot killed during action in the Pacific Ocean.

and down the Illinois, Mississippi, and Ohio Rivers. They carry Illinois crops and goods to market.

In the late 1800s, Illinois became the world's greatest railroad center. Railroads from all over the country met in Illinois. Trains still carry people and products to and from Illinois. In fact, Illinois trains carry over 450 million tons (408 metric tons) of freight each year.

In the late 1900s, Illinois was the destination for more air travelers than any other place in the world.

Hundreds of years ago, rivers carried travelers and goods to Illinois. Today, interstate highways do the job. Illinois has more than 20,000 miles (32,000 kilometers) of interstate highways.

Illinois Transportation

Northern

Galena
Rockford
Byron
Greater Rockford Airport
Elgin
Waukegan
Arlington Heights
Des Plaines
Evanston
Skokie
Chicago O'Hare Int'l Airport
Oak Park
Chicago
Wheaton
Dixon
Aurora
Naperville
Joliet
Chicago Midway Airport
Illinois & Michigan Canal
Moline
Rock Island
Quad City Int'l Airport
Bishop Hill
Tampico
La Salle
Kankakee
Fox River
Mississippi River
Rock River
Illinois River
Kankakee River

Galesburg

Central

Nauvoo
Peoria
Greater Peoria Regional Airport
Pekin
Bloomington
Eureka
Normal
Central IL Regional Airport at Bloomington/Normal
Champaign
Urbana
Danville
Quincy
New Salem
Capital Airport
Springfield
Decatur Airport
Arthur
Lake Shelbyville
Mattoon
Sangamon River
Illinois River
Kaskaskia River
Embarras River

Godfrey
Alton
St. Louis Regional Airport
Vandalia
Effingham
East St. Louis
Cahokia
Edwardsville
Carlyle Lake
Centralia
Mt. Vernon
Grayville
Mid-America Airport
Prairie du Rocher
Rend Lake
Kaskaskia
Williamson County Regional Airport
Shawneetown
Wabash River
Mississippi River

Southern

Carbondale
Big Muddy River
Cairo
Ohio River

Legend

— Interstate Highways
— State Highways
+—+ Railroad Lines
+—+ Railroad Connecting Lines
✈ Airports

0   50 mi.
0   50 km

Chicago's O'Hare International Airport earned the title "world's busiest airport." More than 65 million travelers use O'Hare each year. Illinois is also home to another 1,000 airports and landing strips of all sizes.

State and interstate highways also connect Illinois to the world. Illinois is fourth in the country in miles of road. It boasts more than 20,000 miles (32,000 kilometers) of interstate highways. It has another 34,000 miles (54,000 kilometers) of state highways.

Illinois has many miles of highways and railroad tracks, as well as several airports. It is a center for transportation in the United States.

Northern Illinois

The area we know as northern Illinois almost became part of Wisconsin. Before Illinois became a state in 1818, the United States Congress had to set Illinois's borders. Originally, Illinois's northern border was supposed to be near the southern tip of Lake Michigan. However, an Illinois leader named Daniel Pope Cook convinced Congress to redraw the map of the new state. Congress moved the border 41 miles (66 kilometers) north, to its present position. Cook County, Illinois, was named in Cook's honor.

The area of Illinois added by Congress became very important to the state's development. That area includes the beautiful Apple River Valley of northwest Illinois. It also includes most of Illinois's Lake Michigan shoreline. That shoreline helped connect Illinois to the rest of the Great Lakes and eastern United States. The northern region

The northwest part of the state is full of rolling hills (below), as well as the state's highest point: Charles Mound.

also includes Galena, the home of the eighteenth president of the United States, Ulysses S. Grant.

It includes part of the Rock River Valley, the childhood home of Ronald Reagan, the 40th president of the United States. It also includes Chicago, by far the biggest city in the state and the third largest in the nation.

LAND AND WATER

Northern Illinois includes the state's highest point. It is also home to some of the lowest-lying land in the state. In between are smaller hills, valleys, and bits of the prairies that once covered Illinois.

Illinois's highest point is Charles Mound in Jo Daviess County. It is located in the northwest corner of the state. This area is one of three "driftless areas" of Illinois, or areas that were never covered by **glaciers.** As a result, the land there has not been flattened by the actions of glaciers. Instead, it is marked by small but steep slopes.

Across the state, northeast Illinois has a very different natural history. It is the area of Illinois that was most recently covered by glaciers. The last of the glaciers melted away about 15,000 years ago. The melting water of that

Northern Illinois Topography

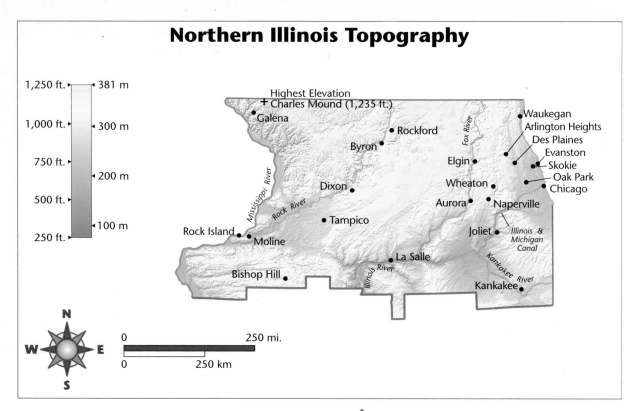

Northern Illinois contains Charles Mound, the highest point in the state at 1,235 feet. It also contains hilly land, important rivers, the Lake Michigan shoreline, and Chicago, the largest city in the state.

glacier formed a huge lake that covered the site where Chicago stands today. Eventually, the water drained away down ancient rivers to the Gulf of Mexico. Today, Chicago and other parts of northeast Illinois stand on what used to be the bed of that ancient lake. The land there is very flat and lower than other parts of Illinois. Some of Chicago was even built on what used to be swampland.

Much of north-central Illinois is flat, too. However, there are areas of gentle slopes and ridges. These ridges are called **moraines.** They are piles of ground-up rock and dirt left behind by glaciers. One of the largest moraines in Illinois is the Bloomington Moraine. It is a C-shaped ridge that runs from just north of DeKalb to just east of Bloomington.

Northern Illinois contains some beautiful river valleys. The Apple River Valley Canyon formed as waters of the Apple River cut through **limestone** over thousands of years. This process is called **erosion.** In a similar way,

Midewin National Tallgrass Prairie

Much of northern Illinois was once home to vast prairies. Bits of prairie can still be found in the region. The Midewin National Tallgrass Prairie is one of the biggest prairie preserves in the state. A preserve is a place where **conservation** of the land and its **resources** is practiced. Midewin is located near Joliet, on the site of a former U.S. Army plant. It was replanted with native prairie grasses, like those that once covered Illinois. Today, it offers a glimpse of the kind of land that settlers in the early 1800s found in Illinois.

the Pecatonica River cut steep canyons that are up to 250 feet (76 meters) deep.

Northern Illinois rivers have played an important role in the state's history. The Chicago and Des Plaines Rivers were part of the route that carried French traders from Canada to the Mississippi River in the late 1600s. However, northern Illinois wasn't settled for another 150 years. When settlers did come to the region, they settled along the rivers. In the 1820s, steamboats on the Mississippi River began to serve the booming mining town of Galena. In the 1830s, settlers from New England and New York began to settle along the Fox and Rock Rivers.

Canals also helped northern Illinois grow. In 1848, the Illinois and Michigan Canal opened between Chicago and LaSalle. This made it possible for boats and **barges** to

The Apple River Canyon (right) was formed by water from the Apple River cutting through limestone over thousands of years in a process called erosion.

Illinois and Michigan Canal

Native Americans and early French explorers used both Lake Michigan and the Illinois River as water highways. They paddled their canoes through the lake and into the Chicago River. Then they portaged, or carried, their canoes overland to the Des Plaines River, just a few miles west. The Des Plaines River then led them to the Illinois River.

However, parts of those rivers were not wide enough or deep enough to carry boats much larger than canoes. So in 1836, construction began on the Illinois and Michigan Canal. When it was completed in 1848, it connected Chicago and LaSalle. It allowed **barges** loaded with goods to travel by water all the way across Illinois. The canal helped spur the growth of northern Illinois. Chicago grew quickly in the decade after the canal opened. The canal is now a state park (above).

travel across the state, from the Mississippi River to Lake Michigan. The canal helped make Chicago a center for Illinois trade. Today, the canal is a state park lined with nature preserves and historic sites.

NATURAL RESOURCES

Many of northern Illinois's first settlers came to mine lead near Galena. The lead mines of northwest Illinois became one of the state's first **industries.** They also helped make Galena a successful town. One of the primary uses of lead was in the making of bullets.

Later, **limestone quarries** and clay pits across northern Illinois provided building materials for growing cities. Crushed stone and gravel from northern Illinois still help supply builders of roads and **suburbs.**

One of northern Illinois's greatest natural **resources** is underground water. Much of northern Illinois draws its drinking water from wells that bring water up from deep under the ground.

CLIMATE

Northern Illinois experiences cold, dry winters and warm, humid summers. Areas near Lake Michigan are the most humid during the summer months. Compared to other parts of Illinois, the north gets less yearly rainfall. About 34 inches (86 centimeters) of rain

Northern Illinois has a wide variety of resources. The northwest corner has long been known as a source of lead. Most manufacturing takes place around the Chicago area.

Northern Illinois Resources

Natural Resources
- Stone, gravel

Agriculture
- Hay
- Beef
- Corn
- Dairy products
- Hogs
- Sheep

Manufacturing
- Steel
- Lead
- Farm equipment
- Food products
- Electrical machinery/equipment

0   50 mi.

0   50 km

Winter snowstorms can dump inches of snow in northern Illinois. Blizzards (above) can make getting around Chicago a more difficult experience.

will fall in a typical year in northern Illinois. That compares to about 46 inches (117 centimeters) of rain in southern Illinois. Northern Illinois gets less rainfall because it is farther from the Gulf of Mexico. Much of the rainfall in Illinois begins as water vapor from the Gulf of Mexico that travels north in clouds. However, northern Illinois sees more snowstorms than other parts of the state. About 30 inches (76 centimeters) of snow fall in a typical winter.

Like other parts of the state, northern Illinois is hit by tornadoes. Tornadoes are rotating funnels of air that move from thunderstorm clouds to the ground. They are powerful enough to destroy buildings and property. Tornadoes have killed more than 1,000 people in Illinois since 1916.

The growing season in northern Illinois is about 155 days long, beginning in May and running until October. The growing season is the period during which an area experiences no frost. Frost is made of tiny droplets of ice that cover plants, often killing them. On a typical winter day in northern Illinois, the temperature is about

Illinois Precipitation

Average Yearly Precipitation

Inches	Centimeters
More than 44	More than 112
40 to 44	102 to 112
36 to 40	91 to 102
Less than 36	Less than 91

22° Fahrenheit (-6° Celsius). On a typical summer day, it's about 74° Fahrenheit (23° Celsius).

INDUSTRY

Illinois business and **industry** is dominated by Chicago and its **suburbs.** Chicago is the Midwest's leading financial center. It is the home of many banks, insurance companies, and companies that provide financial services. Chicago is also home to many manufacturing

The southern tip of Illinois gets the most rain each year. However, northern Illinois gets more snow than the rest of the state.

This is a rare quiet moment at the Chicago Board of Trade at the end of La Salle Street in Chicago. Usually the area is bustling with traffic as traders work within. Chicago is the Midwest's leading financial center.

companies. Seven of every ten Illinois jobs in the manufacturing industry are in the Chicago area. The city and suburbs are leading producers of metal products and electronics. Chicago is the third largest center for printing and publishing in the United States. The Chicago area is also the home of some of the world's best-known food producers. Their products include baked goods from Sara Lee, Wrigley's chewing gum, and Kraft cheese. Many of the country's biggest companies have headquarters in Chicago or its suburbs. These include McDonald's, Sears Roebuck, United Airlines, Boeing, Dean Foods, Quaker Oats, and Motorola.

Of course, there are other business centers in northern Illinois. Rockford companies are leading producers of machine tools and auto parts. The Quad Cities of western Illinois are home to several companies that make farm equipment. The Quad Cities include Moline, East Moline, Rock Island, and Davenport, which is located just across the Mississippi River in Iowa. Deere and Company of Moline is one of Illinois's oldest businesses. It was founded in 1837 by John Deere, a **blacksmith** who invented the first successful steel plow.

AGRICULTURE

Northern Illinois is home to Illinois's largest cities. However, most of the region is still covered by farms.

John Deere changed Illinois with the invention of his simple, steel plow in 1837. Today, John Deere and Company makes more advanced farm machinery (left) in Moline. It is one of Illinois's oldest businesses.

Like other parts of the state, northern Illinois is a leading corn producer. Corn grown there is sold all over the United States and the world. Some of the corn is used as feed grain for farm animals. Fields of grass and clover in northern Illinois are turned into hay for farm animals. In Ogle and DeKalb Counties, farmers also grow pumpkins.

Northern Illinois farmers also raise a variety of livestock animals. Sheep are raised in the hilly western sections for wool. Hogs and beef cattle are raised for meat and other products. Henry County is Illinois's leading hog producer. In the far northern sections of Illinois, dairy farms produce milk and cheese.

Harvard Milk Days

Harvard is the home of Harmilda, a life-size fiberglass cow that stands at the center of town. Harmilda (left) is named for Harvard Milk Days, a celebration held every year in June. It includes a parade and milk-drinking contests.

CITIES

Northern Illinois is home to eight of Illinois's ten largest cities. Chicago is by far the biggest city in Illinois. When Chicago became a city in 1833, it had just 350 residents. Sixty years later, Chicago's population was one million. After fifty years of declining populations, Chicago is growing again. In 2000, Chicago's population stood at 2,896,014. Chicago is world famous for its beautiful buildings and lakefront parks. It is also the Midwest's capital of business and **industry.** Only New York City is home to more major corporations.

Many of Chicago's **suburbs** are growing, as well. Aurora has grown to become Illinois's third largest city. Its population is 142,990. Naperville is now the fourth largest city in Illinois, with 128,358 people. All around the Chicago area, new homes and businesses are being built on land that was once farmland.

Many of Chicago's suburbs are growing fast. People move from cities into new homes like these (below) partly to have more space, backyards, and garages. Today, suburban homes are often more affordable as well.

Major corporations like McDonald's and Baxter International have their headquarters in Chicago's suburbs. McDonald's restaurants are located in 120 countries around the world. Baxter International is a world leader in producing medicines and treatments for sick people.

Rockford grew up around a ford—or place to cross a river—on the Rock River. Settlers built **mills** there that provided power for the city's furniture-making industry. Today, Rockford is Illinois's second largest city, with more than 150,000 people.

Rock Island, Moline, and East Moline are three of the four Quad Cities. (Davenport, Iowa, is the fourth.) The Quad Cities are located along either side of the Mississippi River. Rock Island was the site of the first railroad bridge across the Mississippi River, built in 1856.

Lead mines helped make Galena (above) a prosperous town in the 1830s and 1840s. Today it is a popular tourist destination where people visit Grant's home and shop for antiques.

Galena was Illinois's first **boomtown.** Area mines supplied much of the nation's lead in the 1830s and 1840s. (Galena is actually also the name of a kind of lead.) The lead was shipped from Galena all over the country on steamboats that worked the Mississippi River. In the early 1800s, Galena was the richest town in Illinois. Today, people visit Galena to admire the city's grand old houses, shop for antiques, and visit the home of Ulysses S. Grant, Civil War general and the eighteenth president of the United States.

Central Illinois

Central Illinois has some of the world's richest farmland. It was once part of one of the largest prairies in the world. A person standing in the middle of the central Illinois prairie in the 1800s might see only tall grass in all directions. Many early pioneers compared it to being on a ship in the middle of the ocean. They called the prairie a sea of grass.

Central Illinois is no longer covered with tall prairie grass. Almost all of the prairies have been replaced by farms. The crops grown there are **exported** all over the world. Today, a person standing in a central Illinois field might see nothing but corn stalks in all directions.

However, visitors to central Illinois will also find scenic rivers lined with rocky **bluffs.** They will find lively cities and huge universities. And, on central Illinois's human-made lakes, they will see people boating and fishing.

Within 200 years, the vast prairies of central Illinois have been turned into vast fields of corn, soybeans, and other farm crops.

LAND AND WATER

Central Illinois is the flattest part of the state. However, anyone who has ever tried to ride a bike there knows it's not perfectly flat. There are gentle slopes that rise to form ridges. These ridges are called **moraines.** They were formed by melting **glaciers** about 20,000 years ago. When the glaciers melted they left behind piles of ground-up rock that formed the moraines. Several large moraines stretch across northern and central Illinois. Moraine View State Recreation Area is located on one of these moraines, just east of Bloomington.

Between moraines there are stretches of low-lying land. During rainy periods, water can collect and turn the land into swampy bogs. Before this land could be successfully farmed, settlers had to drain it. They dug ditches that carried extra water away. In some parts of east-central Illinois, land was not fully drained for farming until around 1900.

Along the Mississippi River in central Illinois, the land becomes hilly. This was one of the few areas of Illinois that was not made flat by the actions of ancient glaciers. One of the hilly sections is in Calhoun County, between the Mississippi and Illinois Rivers. Calhoun County sits on top of **karst** formations. Karst is **limestone** that is softened by water until it grows weak. Sometimes karst

Peoria (above) is the oldest city in central Illinois. In fact, the French explorer La Salle built a fort near the site in the 1600s. Today, Peoria is the fifth most populated city in Illinois.

cracks and swallows trees and other parts of the land-scape in large **sinkholes.**

Central Illinois's major rivers are the Kaskaskia, Illinois, Embarras, Vermillion, Mackinaw, and Sangamon. The first **forts** and trading posts built by French explorers in Illinois were along the Illinois River. After Illinois became a state in 1818, many early settlers lived along the rivers of central Illinois. On the riverbanks, they found timber for their fences and houses. They used the rivers themselves to float their farm produce to market on **flatboats.**

Central Illinois is home to few natural lakes. One of them, Lake Peoria, was the subject of cleanup efforts to rid it of pollution that was harming the wildlife. The central region has several human-made lakes. These include Lake Decatur and Lake Shelbyville.

Lake Shelbyville is one of the human-made lakes of central Illinois. Construction of a dam (below) there began in 1963. It was meant to control flooding in the area.

Central Illinois Topography

1,250 ft. — 381 m
1,000 ft. — 300 m
750 ft. — 200 m
500 ft. — 100 m
250 ft.

Galesburg
Illinois River
Peoria
Pekin
Eureka
Nauvoo
Normal
Bloomington
Quincy
Champaign
Danville
Urbana
Sangamon River
Embarras River
New Salem
Springfield
Arthur
Lake Shelbyville
Mattoon
Mississippi River
Illinois River
Kaskaskia River
Wabash River

0 — 250 mi.
0 — 250 km

RESOURCES

Central Illinois's greatest **resource** is its rich farm soil. Beneath the soil, central Illinois also offers **mineral resources. Limestone** is gathered for use as a building material. Farmers also add limestone to some kinds of soil to make it more **fertile.** Some of Illinois's vast coal reserves are in central Illinois. So are the sand and gravel that are mined for use in building new homes and highways. Underground water is another valuable resource. Wells pumping water from under the ground provide much of Illinois's water. One of the challenges facing central Illinois is keeping its underground water supplies clean. Chemical **fertilizers** used in farming and waste from housing developments can seep through **porous** rock and pollute underground water.

Central Illinois is mostly flat farmland, but there is some variety. Springfield, the state's capital, is located in central Illinois, as are some important rivers.

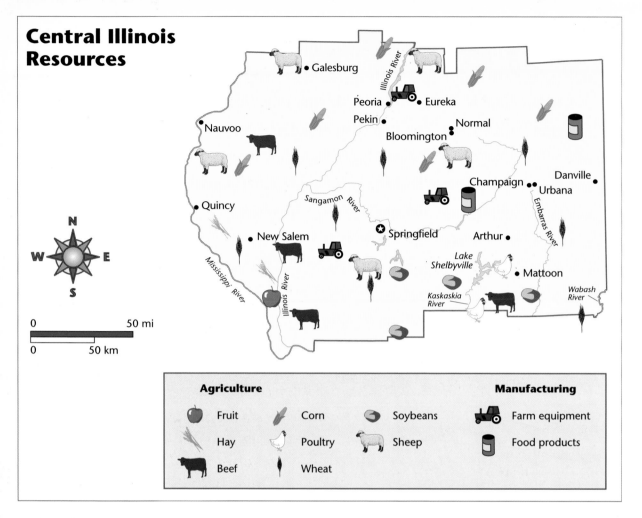

Central Illinois Resources

Agriculture

Fruit Corn Soybeans

Hay Poultry Sheep

Beef Wheat

Manufacturing

Farm equipment

Food products

Central Illinois has a variety of resources. Perhaps the most valuable resource of the region is its farmland. Crops grown in central Illinois are sold all over the world.

CLIMATE

Central Illinois experiences slightly warmer summers than northern Illinois. Its winters are slightly colder and snowier than southern Illinois. Central Illinois receives more freezing rainstorms than either southern or northern Illinois. See the map on page 21 to learn how much rain falls in central Illinois each year. On a typical January day in Springfield, the temperature will be 25° Fahrenheit (-4° Celsius). On a typical July day, it will be 76° Fahrenheit (24° Celsius). The growing season in central Illinois is 188 days long.

A "tornado belt" stretches across central Illinois, from Jersey County on the Mississippi River to Iroquois County on Illinois's eastern border. (It also extends along Lake Michigan in northern Illinois, and south along the Mississippi River in southern Illinois.) This stretch of land experiences the most tornadoes of any part of the state. A tornado that cut across central Illinois on May 26, 1917, killed 101 people. It was one of the ten deadliest tornadoes in Illinois history.

Central Illinois experiences more tornadoes than any other part of the state. Tornadoes can be very dangerous. They have killed more people in Illinois than in any other state.

AGRICULTURE

The first settlers in central Illinois avoided the vast prairies. They thought the huge stretches of tall grass were a wasteland with no value for farming. The prairie land was very hard to prepare for planting. Farmers had to use cast-iron plows that didn't cut through the tough prairie grass roots. In 1837, John Deere invented a steel plow that could help farmers turn over prairie land. By 1847, the plows were being manufactured in Moline. They helped turn the great central Illinois prairie into valuable farmland. By 1900, most of the prairie had been replaced by farms.

The Military Tract

The western part of central Illinois is sometimes called the Military Tract. A tract is a piece of land. The Military Tract lies between the Illinois and Mississippi Rivers. It includes Adams, Brown, Calhoun, Fulton, Hancock, Henderson, Knox, McDonough, Mercer, Peoria, Pike, Schuyler, Stark, and Warren Counties. Beginning in 1817, land there was divided up and given to veterans of the War of 1812 as a reward for their service. Some of the former soldiers came to Illinois to live on their new land. As a result, the western part of central Illinois was settled much earlier than the eastern part.

Corn has been a leading crop in Illinois since Native Americans began growing it 1,200 years ago. Today, McLean County in Illinois is the nation's leading corn-producing county. In the late 1900s, Illinois farmers began growing soybeans, as well. Soybeans come from Asia originally and are used to make soy sauce, tofu, and other foods. They are also used to make products like ink and paint. Champaign County is the country's leading soybean producer.

Wheat is another leading crop, especially in Adams and Pike Counties. Calhoun County is one of the few places in Illinois that grows peaches.

INDUSTRY

Industry in central Illinois is often connected to farming. Decatur is home to two large companies that process farm products.

John Deere's new steel plow (right) helped farmers prepare the grassy soil of central Illinois for planting. It was able to cut cleanly through the tough roots of prairie grasses.

The A.E. Staley Co. makes syrups and other products from corn. Archer Daniels Midland makes animal feed, fuel, and food products from corn, soybeans, and other Illinois crops.

In Peoria, the Caterpillar Company makes trucks and tractors for farming and construction. The Keystone Steel Company in Bartonville began by making wire fences for farmers without easy access to wood. Today, it is a leading manufacturer of steel wire and rods.

Bloomington is home to State Farm Insurance and a large automobile plant. As the state capital, Springfield employs hundreds of people who work in the state government. The University of Illinois in Champaign-Urbana has long been a center of computer technology. The university helped develop a leading program used to explore the **Internet.**

The Caterpillar Company of Peoria is a leading manufacturer of farm equipment (below). It also makes equipment for construction, and is the largest employer in the Peoria area.

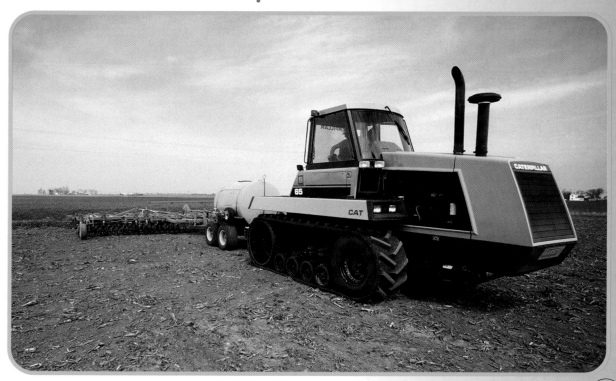

CITIES

Bloomington and Normal sit in the center of Illinois at the junction of three interstate highways. The two cities are home to two of Illinois's oldest colleges. Illinois Wesleyan, in Bloomington, was founded in 1850. Illinois State University in Normal became Illinois's first state-supported college in 1857.

Urbana was founded in 1834. In 1854, the Illinois Central Railroad built a depot two miles west of town. Around that depot, the new city of Champaign quickly grew. The University of Illinois **campus** is spread across both towns. More than 30,000 students from all over the world study at the university.

The University of Illinois is one of the nation's largest state universities. Its main campus (below) is spread across the two towns of Champaign and Urbana in central Illinois.

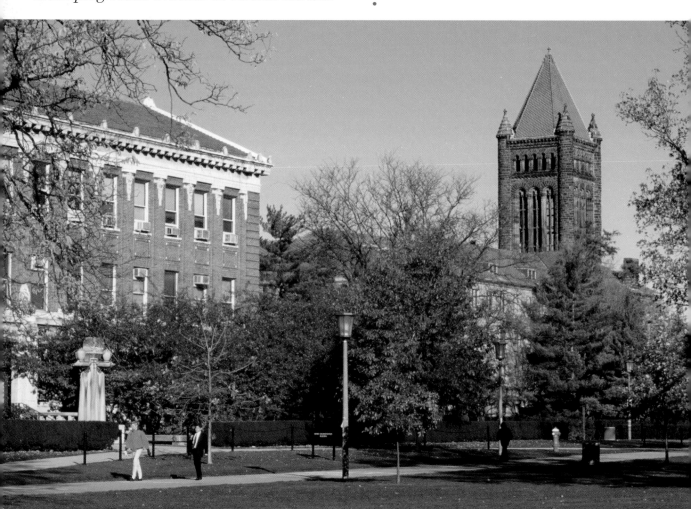